Secondary Selection Portfolio

NON-VERBAL REASONING
General Advice for Pare

What I should know about the practice papers?
The style and methodology of the practice papers in this port   de
practice for children taking similar tests prior to transfer to secondary schools within the state
and private sectors. Five types of non-verbal test are included in the papers, covering the
majority of skills that your child is likely to require. Before your child attempts the papers
work through the examples together so that your child fully understands how to tackle each
of the question types.

How should I administer the practice papers?
To get the most out of the practice papers your child should complete them in the best
possible conditions - a quiet room with good lighting, and not when he is too tired or would
rather be watching a favourite television programme. Any test can be quite threatening - to
adults as well as children. When you are working through the practice examples with your
child ensure that they become familiar with the way their answers must be recorded. Ideally,
you should space out the practice papers so that your child attempts no more that two
papers per week. When you have marked a paper, work through it with your child, looking for
ways to increase his success.

How important is timing?
Each practice paper contains two tests which are individually timed to provide an indication
of the speed required. Provide your child with a clock or watch so that he is able to pace
himself. When the time is up draw a line across the page underneath the last question
completed. Your child should then continue working through the test without being timed so
that he can attempt all the question in that particular test. As a rough guide, children should
complete the whole test within the time limit after they have attempted three or four of the
papers.

How can I help my child to finish the practice papers in the time allowed?
If your child is not completing the practice papers in the time limit it is possible that he is
spending too long puzzling over one particular question. It is far better to attempt a few more
questions and get them right than to spend this time struggling with a question that may in
the end prove too difficult. A second possibility is a lack of appropriate strategy when tackling
a particular type of question. Some children also feel the need to check and double check
their answers before moving on to the next question. Such children tend to be successful
with the questions they attempt but unfortunately are unable to complete the test in the time
allowed. It is far better for children to complete the test and check their answers at the end if
there is still time available.

Marking the test papers
The answers for the six papers in this test pack are on page 4 of this booklet. Total each
page of the test paper and enter the number correct in the grid provided on page 3. Mark
strictly and do not give your child the benefit of the doubt if the answer is difficult to read or
'almost' right.

Further advice send support
For further advice and support visit our extensive website (the password is '105'). As well as lots
of general information for parents there are worked examples of non-verbal question types,
sample papers to download and online timed tests for your children.

Multiple-Choice Question Papers

Selection test papers can be either 'standard' papers or 'multiple-choice' papers. You may have been told which of these papers your child will be given. Both papers contain the same questions. The difference between these two types of paper is the way your child will have to record his or her answers.

The following questions are typical questions from a 'standard' paper.

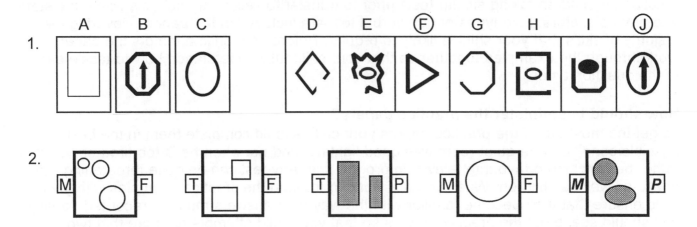

In the first question the child has to find two similar figures to the figures in boxes A, B and C and then circle the letters above these figures as shown. In the second question the child has to work out the code and write the code letters in the last box.

The children's papers are marked by hand. This is a very time consuming process - for some Grammar Schools as many as 1,500 children take the test! So, some schools are now using so-called 'multiple-choice' papers.

The term 'multiple-choice' is not really an accurate way of describing the difference between the two types of paper. As you can see from the examples above, 'standard' papers contain multiple-choice questions! In the first question above the child has to circle two answers from a set of alternatives, ie they have a 'multiple-choice'.

So-called 'multiple-choice' papers are really 'optically marked' papers. Children record their answers on a separate sheet by placing a mark inside a box. This sheet can then be fed into a computer and marked by the computer in a few seconds. The completed answers for the questions above would look like this -

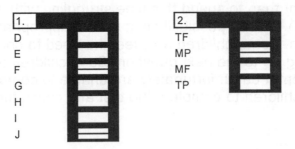

So, as you can see, there is little for you or your child to be concerned about. Of course, your child needs to be familiar with 'multiple-choice' answer papers. However, it is equally important to have sufficient experience of the variety of questions that can crop up. Our Non-Verbal Reasoning Test Pack 7 listed on the back cover will provide this experience. (Please note that the questions in this multiple-choice test pack are from our Non-Verbal Reasoning Test Pack 4)

Finally, do remember to be encouraging and positive with your child. They will be more successful if they know you are pleased with their progress.

Paper 1

PAGE	1	2	3	4	TOTAL
POSSIBLE	6	8	8	9	31
ACTUAL					

Paper 2

PAGE	1	2	3	4	TOTAL
POSSIBLE	7	9	6	7	29
ACTUAL					

Paper 3

PAGE	1	2	3	4	TOTAL
POSSIBLE	5	7	8	9	29
ACTUAL					

Paper 4

PAGE	1	2	3	4	TOTAL
POSSIBLE	7	9	7	8	31
ACTUAL					

Paper 5

PAGE	1	2	3	4	TOTAL
POSSIBLE	5	7	6	7	25
ACTUAL					

Paper 6

PAGE	1	2	3	4	TOTAL
POSSIBLE	7	9	8	9	33
ACTUAL					

Answers

Paper 1

Analogic
Relationships
1. B
2. A
3. E
4. D
5. E
6. B
7. A
8. B
9. E
10. C
11. D
12. C
13. D
14. B

Serial
Relationships
1. B
2. D
3. B
4. E
5. A
6. B
7. A
8. C
9. C
10. C
11. A
12. B
13. D
14. B
15. A
16. E
17. D

Paper 2

Codes
1. XF
2. KP
3. LP
4. PX
5. KD
6. WS
7. PF
8. KP
9. CX
10. BY
11. NF
12. TP
13. RM
14. TF
15. SP
16. LB

Isomorphic
Relationships
1. B and D
2. D and F
3. E and G
4. C and E
5. B and E
6. B and F
7. F and G
8. B and D
9. C and E
10. A and D
11. C and D
12. B and G
13. E and G

Paper 3

Matrices
1. B
2. D
3. E
4. C
5. E
6. C
7. A
8. B
9. D
10. E
11. C
12. E

Serial
Relationships
1. B
2. C
3. E
4. A
5. D
6. B
7. C
8. E
9. E
10. B
11. B
12. B
13. C
14. E
15. A
16. E
17. E

Paper 4

Codes
1. RF
2. RP
3. VT
4. CF
5. DY
6. GP
7. XE
8. HC
9. AP
10. AP
11. ZP
12. ZB
13. AX
14. KS
15. SJ
16. GC

Analogic
Relationships
1. B
2. A
3. B
4. E
5. B
6. E
7. A
8. C
9. E
10. B
11. D
12. E
13. C
14. E
15. E

Paper 5

Matrices
1. A
2. D
3. C
4. A
5. E
6. D
7. E
8. C
9. E
10. D
11. B
12. A

Isomorphic
Relationships
1. B and F
2. A and C
3. C and F
4. A and E
5. F and G
6. B and F
7. C and F
8. B and D
9. D and F
10. F and G
11. A and E
12. D and G
13. A and G

Paper 6

Codes
1. MP
2. KP
3. EX
4. TN
5. TS
6. WU
7. TF
8. TP
9. TA
10. QG
11. DF
12. AP
13. TA
14. KX
15. TP
16. KS

Serial
Relationships
1. B
2. D
3. A
4. C
5. E
6. B
7. E
8. A
9. E
10. B
11. B
12. A
13. A
14. B
15. C
16. B
17. B

Published by
Athey Educational
Tibthorpe East Yorkshire YO25 9LA

☎ 01377 229320

www.athey-educational.co.uk

NON-VERBAL REASONING

Multiple-Choice Question Paper 4

Time allowed - 8 mins

Codes

In these questions there are five boxes containing shapes or patterns. There are two letters at the edge of each of the first four boxes. These letters are a code for the shapes or patterns in each box. Work out the code and find the two-letter code for the last box. There is a different code for each question

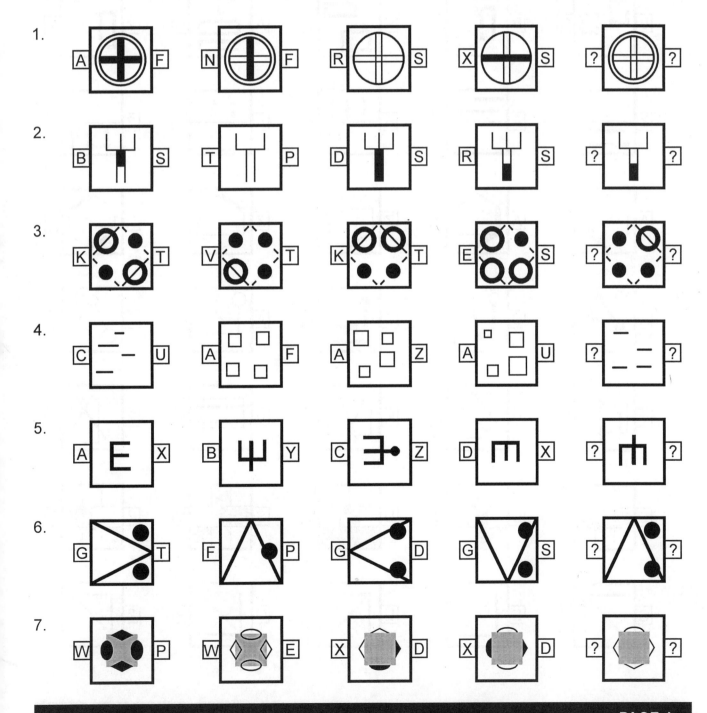

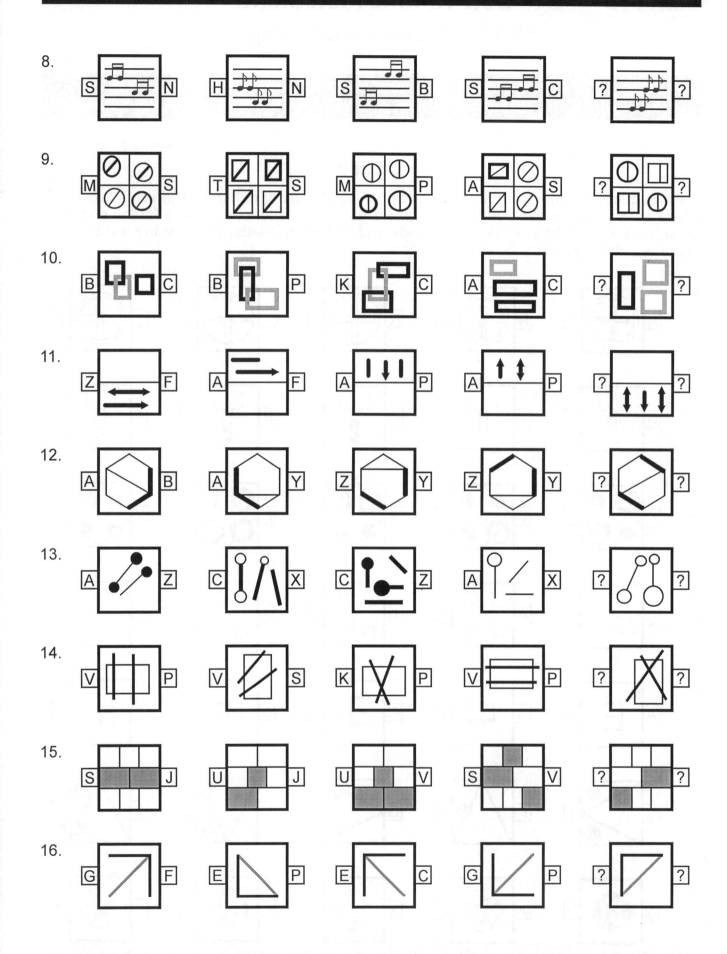

Time allowed - 8 mins

Analogic Relationships

In each of these questions compare the figure in the first box with the figure in the second box. Then look at the figure in the third box and find its partner in the boxes on the right.

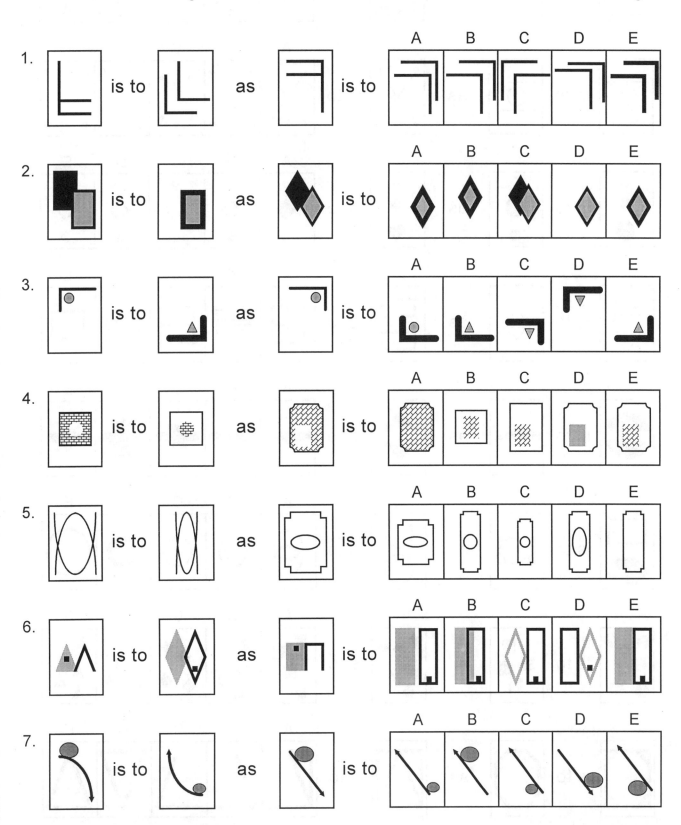

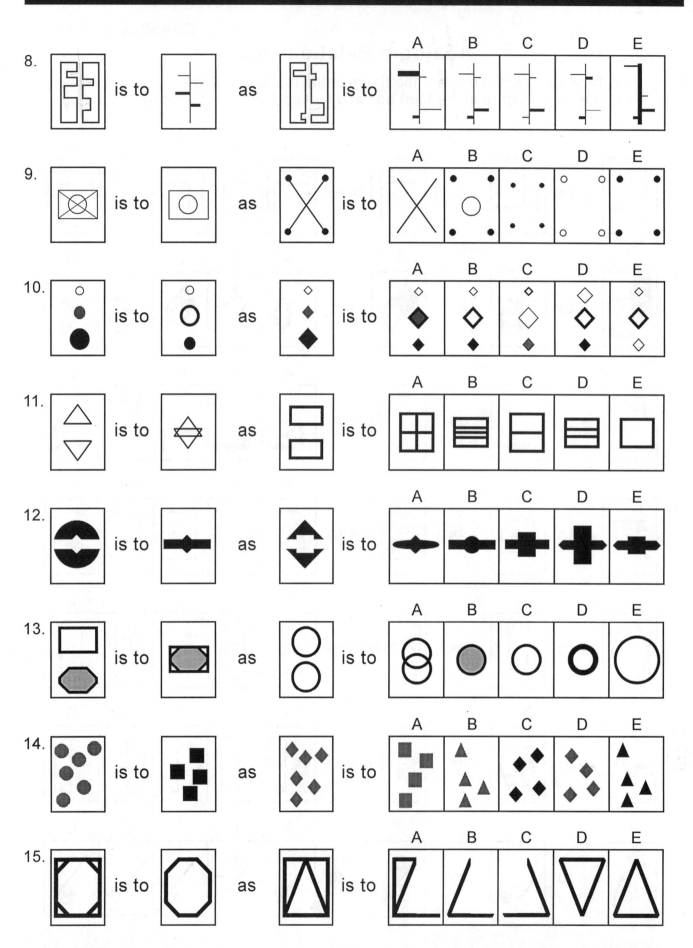

Copyright 1999   Athey Educational

Secondary Selection Portfolio

NON-VERBAL REASONING
Test Pack 4
Multiple-Choice Version

Answer Booklet

Please read the instructions carefully
before starting a practice paper

INSTRUCTIONS

1. There are two sections in each test paper. Start working at the beginning of each section and work straight through.
2. These tests are multiple-choice. Your answers have to be entered on the answer sheet.
3. Work in pencil. You will also need a rubber.
4. Draw a line through the box next to your answer. If you need to change your answer rub it out and enter your new answer.
5. Note that some questions require more than one answer.
6. Answer the questions as quickly and as accurately as you can.
7. If you find you cannot answer any particular question do not spend too much time on it but move to the next one. Remember, if you finish all the questions on time you can return to any you have left out.
8. If you need to do any rough working you can use the side of the page if you wish.
9. Once you begin you will not be allowed to ask any questions.

Go to our website for online timed tests
www.athey-educational.co.uk

EXAMPLES OF QUESTION TYPES

The following worked examples will prepare you for the tests. There is an example of each question type. Record your answers for these examples at the bottom of page 2.

Analogic Relationships

In these questions the relationship between box A and box B must first be established. The same relationship must then be established between box C and one of the boxes D to H. In the example below, A is a is a straight continuous line. B is a straight line of the same length and width as line A and in the same orientation but is not continuous. Having established the similarities and differences between line A and line B the same relationship should be sought between line C and the possible answers D to H. Find the correct answer.

1.

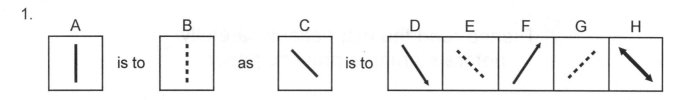

Isomorphic Relationships

In these questions you need to look for similar features in the three boxes on the left and find two boxes on the right with the same similar features. In the example below, the first three boxes contain different shapes with different line thicknesses but each shape is 'closed', ie constructed with a continuous line. If we now look at the possible answers on the right there are only two boxes which contain shapes with these features. Other features, such as the arrows in boxes B and J, are intended to distract you and can be ignored. Which two boxes contain the correct answers?

2.

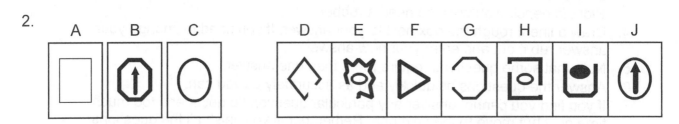

Serial Relationships

In this type of question the boxes on the left contain a 'series', ie a gradually changing or progressing pattern. One of the boxes is empty and you must infer from working out the series which of the possible answers on the right should go in this box. In the following example there is an identical line in each box and a ball on either side of the line. As the series progresses the balls gradually move from one end of the line to the other. Look at the boxes on the right and choose the correct answer.

3.

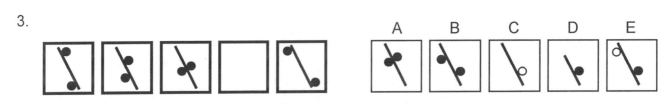

Codes

This type of question asks you to work out the two-letter code associated with a shape or pattern. There are five shapes or patterns and four of these are coded. In the example below, the box with the missing code contains two shaded curved shapes. If we look at the other boxes we can see that two of the boxes contain curved shapes and two contain rectangles. The first letter of the code possibly stands for 'type of shape', ie 'M' for 'curved shape' and 'T' for 'rectangle'. If we now look at the second letter of each code we can see that three of the boxes are coded 'F' and one box, containing the shaded shapes, is coded 'P'. It is probable that 'P' stands for 'shaded shapes' and 'F' stands for 'unshaded shapes'. The number of shapes in each box is not relevant as there is no code that could relate to 'number of shapes'. What is the missing code in this example?

4.

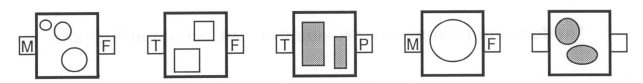

Matrices

In these questions there are rules connecting the shapes or patterns in the large box on the left. When you have worked out the rules, the missing shape or pattern can be selected from the alternatives on the right. In the example below the box at the top left contains two circles, one drawn with a thick line and one with a thin line. The bottom box on the left has an additional circle drawn with a thin line. The top box on the right contains two shapes drawn with thick and thin lines but the shapes are squares. Now find the missing shapes or patterns.

5.

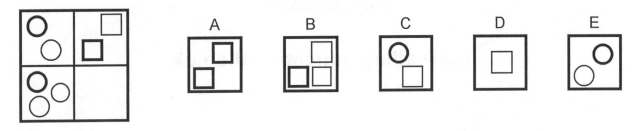

Recording your answers

Draw a line in the box next to your answer as shown in the example on the right.

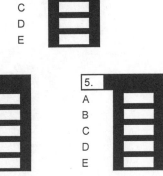

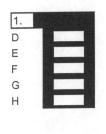

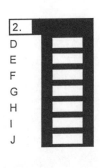

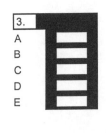

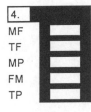

The following support is provided on our customer Website

An explanation of the Grammar School selection process
How to prepare your child
Customer questions answered
Detailed explanations of non-verbal reasoning questions
Multiple choice example papers
An explanation of how selection tests are marked
Standard scores and the effect of age
Online timed tests
and lots more!

www.athey-educational.co.uk

Secondary Selection Portfolio

NON-VERBAL REASONING

Multiple-Choice Answer Paper 1

Analogic Relationships

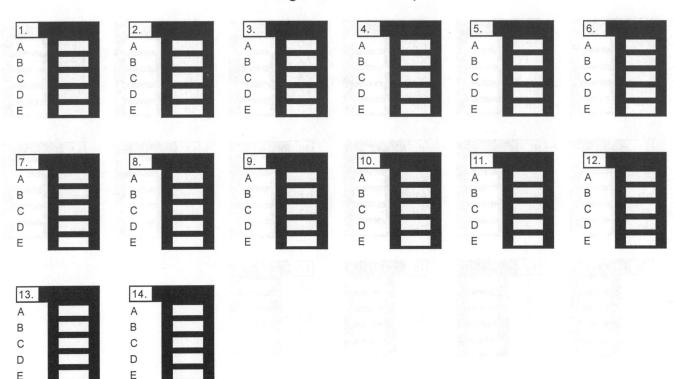

Serial Relationships

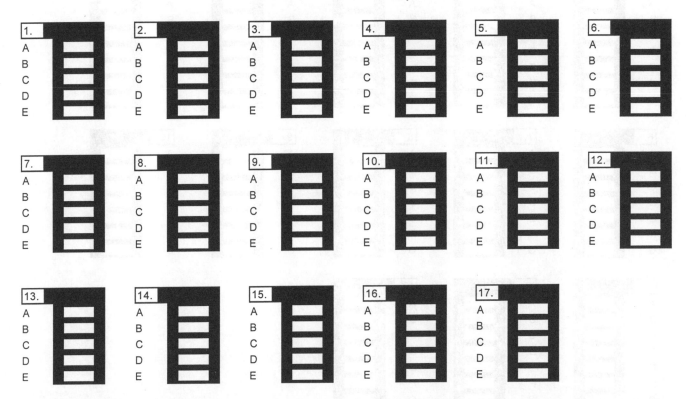

Secondary Selection Portfolio

NON-VERBAL REASONING

Multiple-Choice Answer Paper 2

Codes

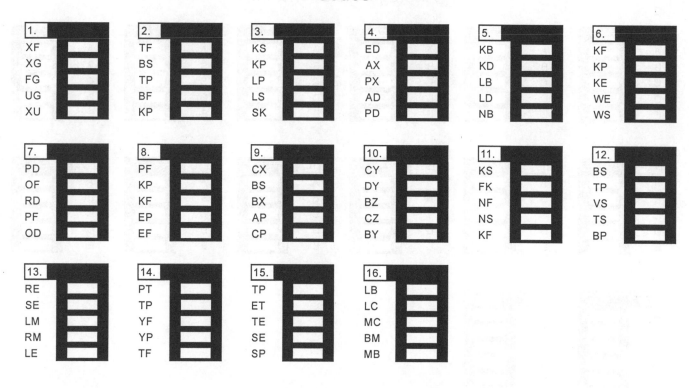

1. XF XG FG UG XU

2. TF BS TP BF KP

3. KS KP LP LS SK

4. ED AX PX AD PD

5. KB KD LB LD NB

6. KF KP KE WE WS

7. PD OF RD PF OD

8. PF KP KF EP EF

9. CX BS BX AP CP

10. CY DY BZ CZ BY

11. KS FK NF NS KF

12. BS TP VS TS BP

13. RE SE LM RM LE

14. PT TP YF YP TF

15. TP ET TE SE SP

16. LB LC MC BM MB

Isomorphic Relationships

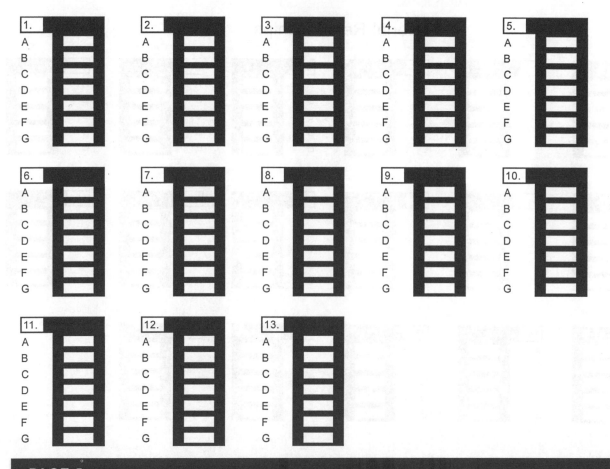

1. A B C D E F G

2. A B C D E F G

3. A B C D E F G

4. A B C D E F G

5. A B C D E F G

6. A B C D E F G

7. A B C D E F G

8. A B C D E F G

9. A B C D E F G

10. A B C D E F G

11. A B C D E F G

12. A B C D E F G

13. A B C D E F G

Secondary Selection Portfolio

NON-VERBAL REASONING

Multiple-Choice Answer Paper 3

Matrices

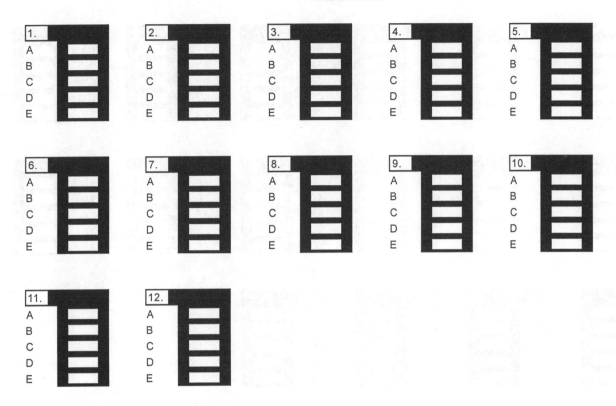

Serial Relationships

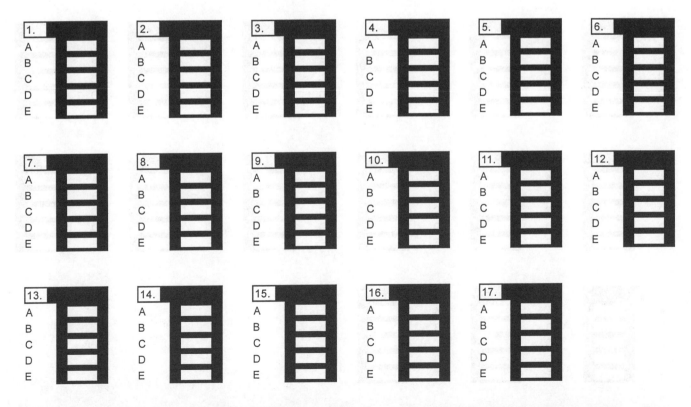

Secondary Selection Portfolio

NON-VERBAL REASONING

Multiple-Choice Answer Paper 4

Codes

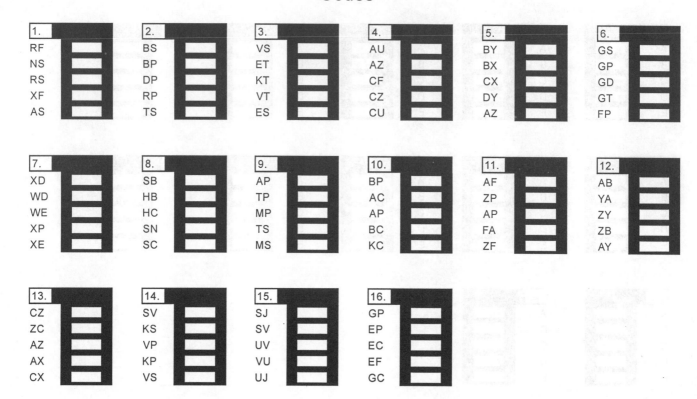

1.	2.	3.	4.	5.	6.
RF	BS	VS	AU	BY	GS
NS	BP	ET	AZ	BX	GP
RS	DP	KT	CF	CX	GD
XF	RP	VT	CZ	DY	GT
AS	TS	ES	CU	AZ	FP

7.	8.	9.	10.	11.	12.
XD	SB	AP	BP	AF	AB
WD	HB	TP	AC	ZP	YA
WE	HC	MP	AP	AP	ZY
XP	SN	TS	BC	FA	ZB
XE	SC	MS	KC	ZF	AY

13.	14.	15.	16.
CZ	SV	SJ	GP
ZC	KS	SV	EP
AZ	VP	UV	EC
AX	KP	VU	EF
CX	VS	UJ	GC

Analogic Relationships

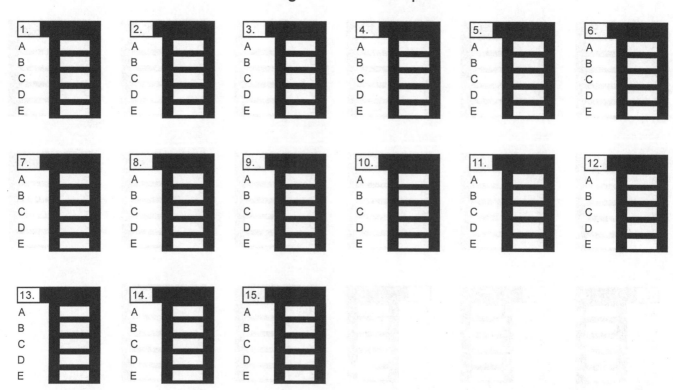

1.	2.	3.	4.	5.	6.
A	A	A	A	A	A
B	B	B	B	B	B
C	C	C	C	C	C
D	D	D	D	D	D
E	E	E	E	E	E

7.	8.	9.	10.	11.	12.
A	A	A	A	A	A
B	B	B	B	B	B
C	C	C	C	C	C
D	D	D	D	D	D
E	E	E	E	E	E

13.	14.	15.
A	A	A
B	B	B
C	C	C
D	D	D
E	E	E

Secondary Selection Portfolio

NON-VERBAL REASONING

Multiple-Choice Answer Paper 5

Matrices

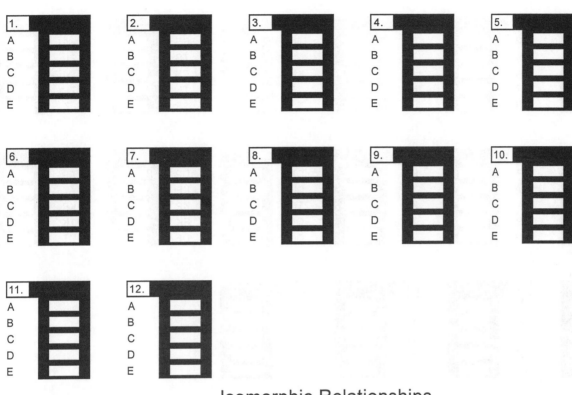

Isomorphic Relationships

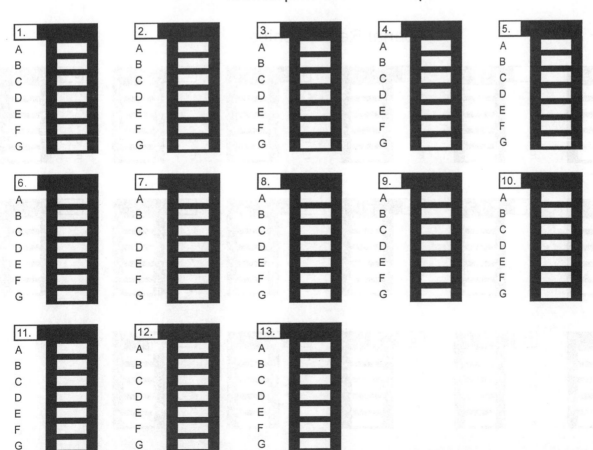

Secondary Selection Portfolio

NON-VERBAL REASONING
Multiple-Choice Answer Paper 6

Codes

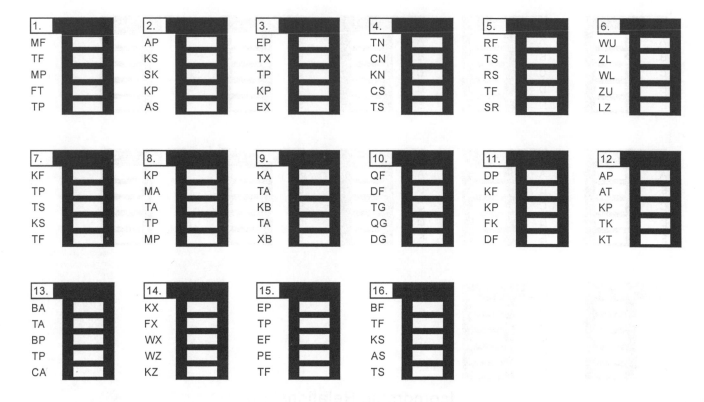

1.	2.	3.	4.	5.	6.
MF	AP	EP	TN	RF	WU
TF	KS	TX	CN	TS	ZL
MP	SK	TP	KN	RS	WL
FT	KP	KP	CS	TF	ZU
TP	AS	EX	TS	SR	LZ

7.	8.	9.	10.	11.	12.
KF	KP	KA	QF	DP	AP
TP	MA	TA	DF	KF	AT
TS	TA	KB	TG	KP	KP
KS	TP	TA	QG	FK	TK
TF	MP	XB	DG	DF	KT

13.	14.	15.	16.
BA	KX	EP	BF
TA	FX	TP	TF
BP	WX	EF	KS
TP	WZ	PE	AS
CA	KZ	TF	TS

Serial Relationships

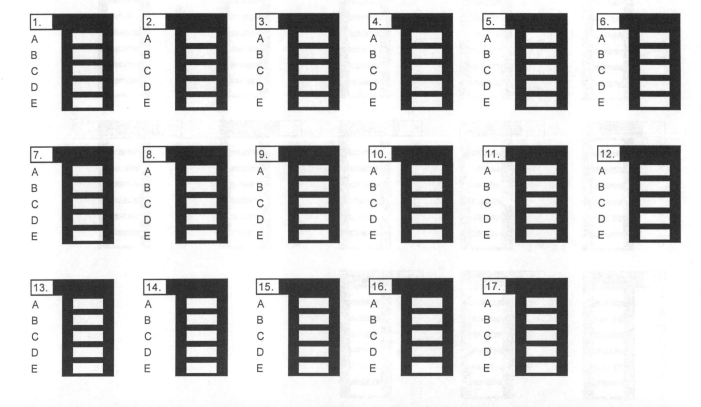

1.	2.	3.	4.	5.	6.
A	A	A	A	A	A
B	B	B	B	B	B
C	C	C	C	C	C
D	D	D	D	D	D
E	E	E	E	E	E

7.	8.	9.	10.	11.	12.
A	A	A	A	A	A
B	B	B	B	B	B
C	C	C	C	C	C
D	D	D	D	D	D
E	E	E	E	E	E

13.	14.	15.	16.	17.
A	A	A	A	A
B	B	B	B	B
C	C	C	C	C
D	D	D	D	D
E	E	E	E	E

Published by
Athey Educational
Tibthorpe East Yorkshire YO25 9LA
☎ 01377 229320
www.athey-educational.co.uk

Secondary Selection Portfolio

NON-VERBAL REASONING
Multiple-Choice Question Paper 1

REMEMBER TO RECORD YOUR ANSWERS ON THE ANSWER PAPER BY DRAWING A LINE THROUGH THE BOX NEXT TO THE ANSWER OR ANSWERS YOU HAVE SELECTED

Time allowed - 7 mins

Analogic Relationships

In each of these questions compare the figure in the first box with the figure in the second box. Then look at the figure in the third box and find its partner in the boxes on the right.

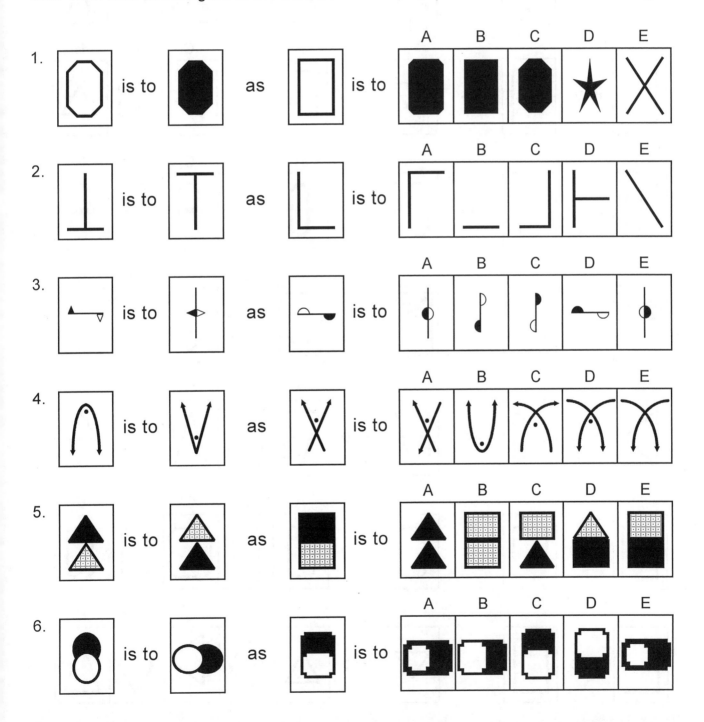

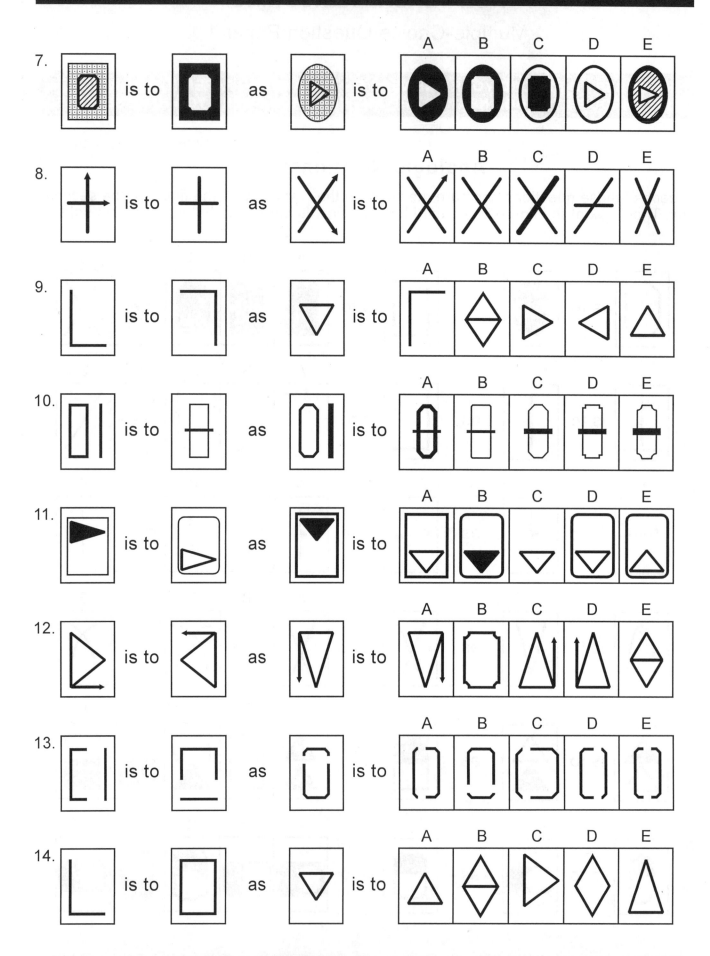

STOP HERE UNTIL YOU ARE TOLD TO CONTINUE

Time allowed - 9 mins

Serial Relationships

In each of the questions below there are five boxes on the left. The figures in these boxes are in order but one is missing. One of the figures in the boxes on the right is the missing figure.

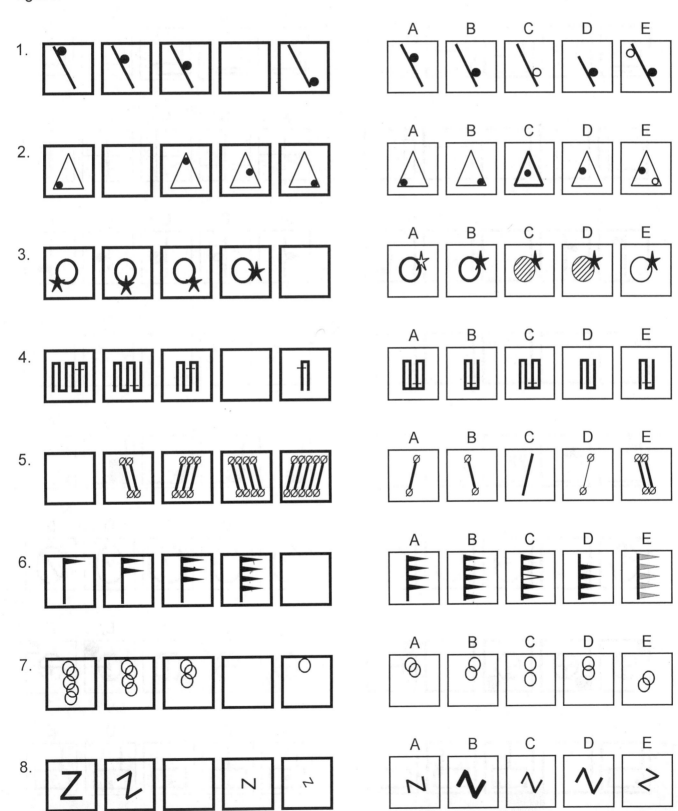

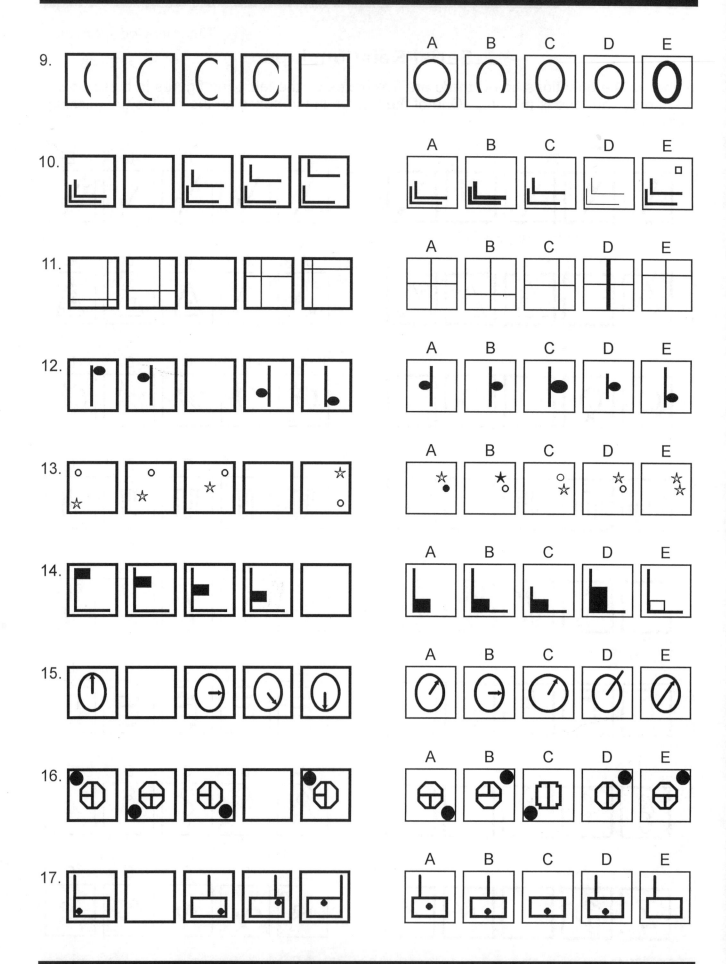

Secondary Selection Portfolio

NON-VERBAL REASONING
Multiple-Choice Question Paper 3

REMEMBER TO RECORD YOUR ANSWERS ON THE ANSWER PAPER BY DRAWING A LINE THROUGH THE BOX NEXT TO THE ANSWER OR ANSWERS YOU HAVE SELECTED

Time allowed - 6 mins

Matrices

In each of the questions below there are four boxes on the left. Three of the boxes contain shapes or patterns. The fourth box is empty. There is a rule connecting the shapes or patterns in each row. There is also a rule for the columns. Work out the rules and choose A, B, C, D or E to show which is the missing shape or pattern.

1.

2.

3.

4.

5.

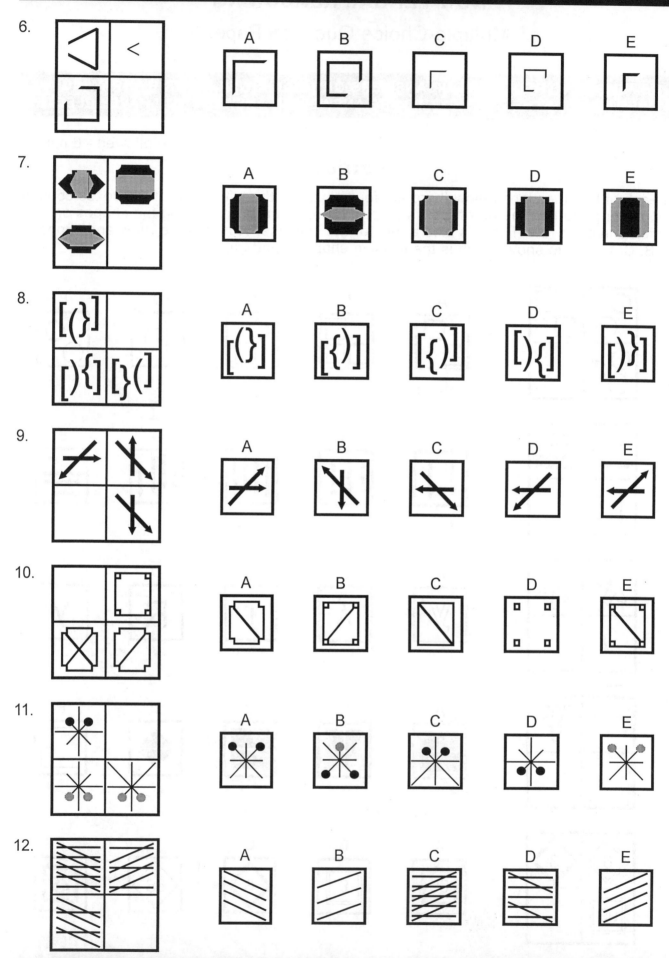

Time allowed - 9 mins

Serial Relationships

In each of the questions below there are five boxes on the left. The figures in these boxes are in order but one is missing. One of the figures in the boxes on the right is the missing figure.

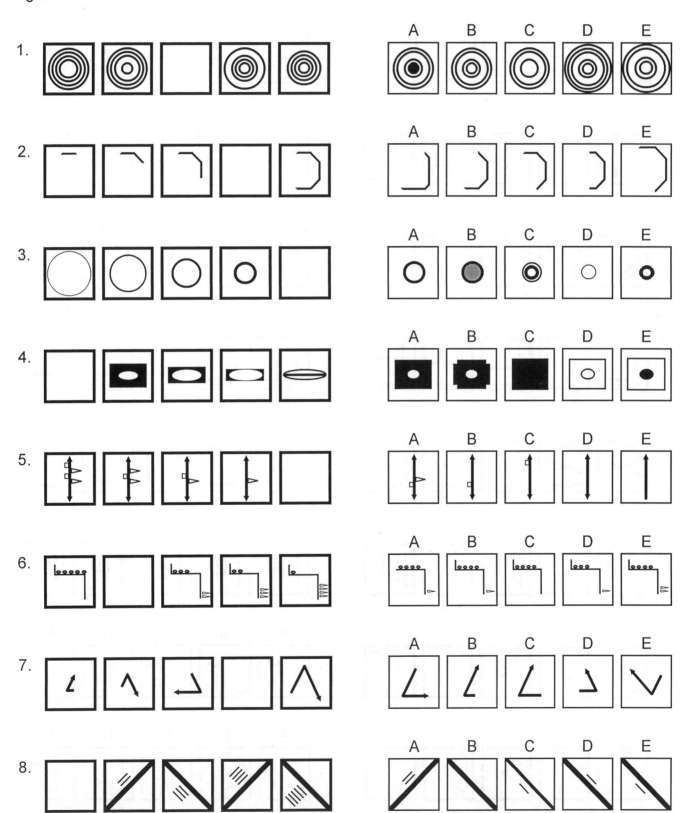

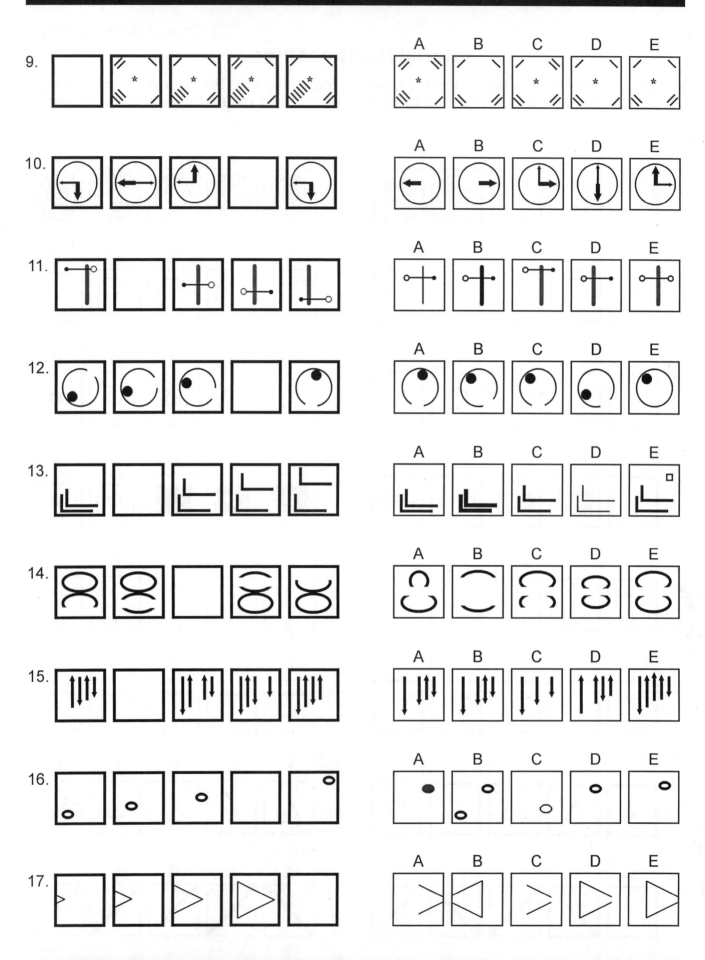

Secondary Selection Portfolio

NON-VERBAL REASONING

Multiple-Choice Question Paper 2

Time allowed - 8 mins

Codes

In these questions there are five boxes containing shapes or patterns. There are two
letters at the edge of each of the first four boxes. These letters are a code for the shapes
or patterns in each box. Work out the code and find the two-letter code for the last box.
There is a different code for each question.

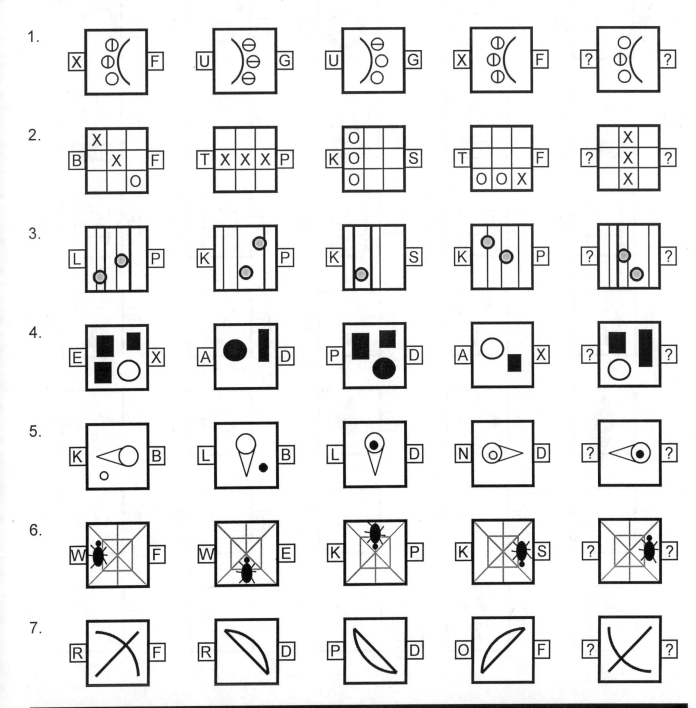

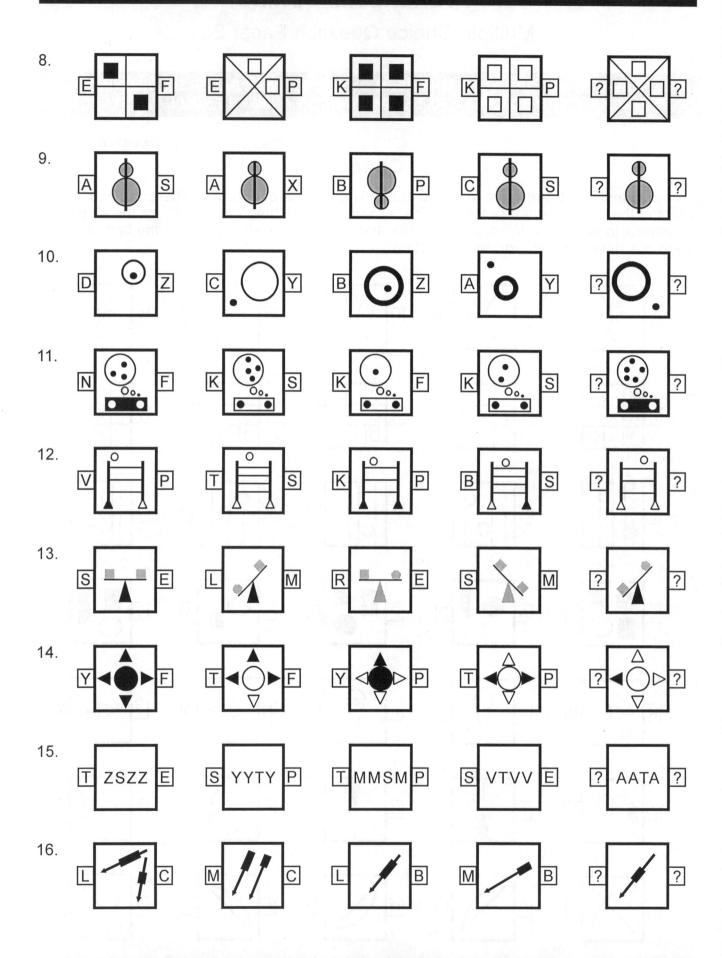

STOP HERE UNTIL YOU ARE TOLD TO CONTINUE

Time allowed - 7 mins

Isomorphic Relationships

In each of these questions the figures in the first three boxes are similar in some way. Look at the shapes in boxes A to G and find **TWO** shapes which are similar to the first three shapes.

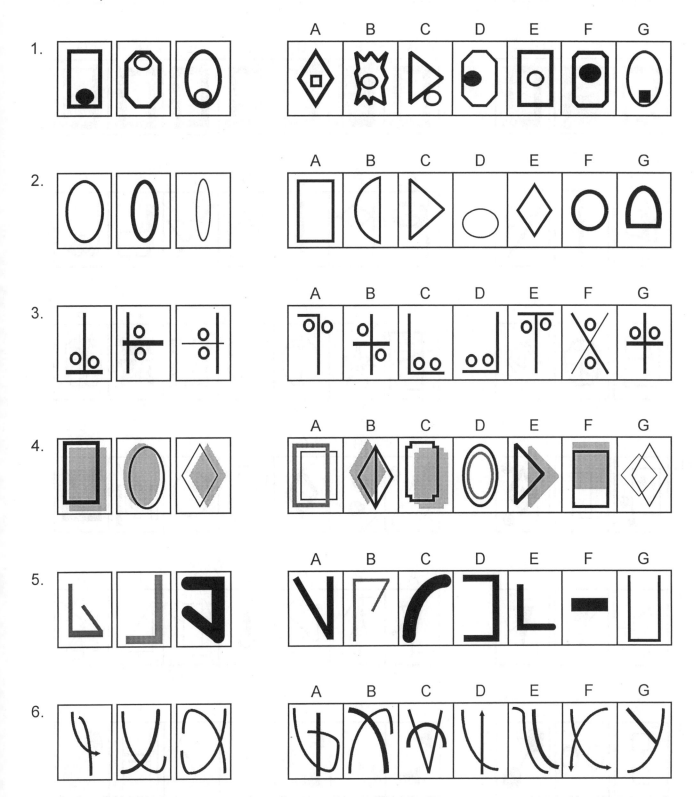

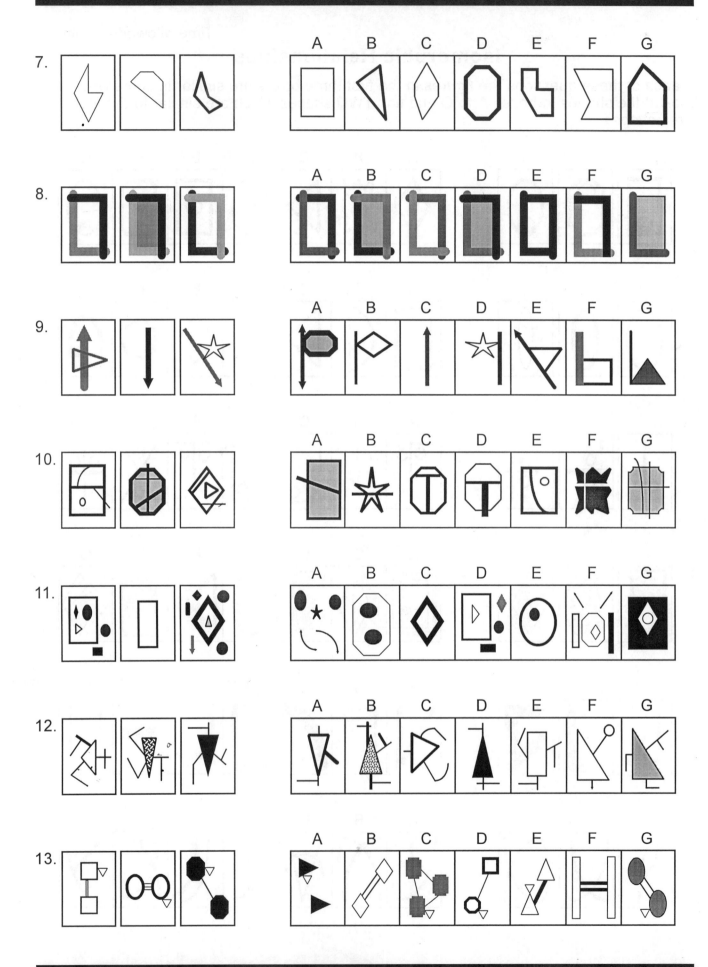

Secondary Selection Portfolio

NON-VERBAL REASONING

Multiple-Choice Question Paper 6

Time allowed - 8 mins

Codes

In these questions there are five boxes containing shapes or patterns. There are two letters at the edge of each of the first four boxes. These letters are a code for the shapes or patterns in each box. Work out the code and find the two-letter code for the last box. There is a different code for each question

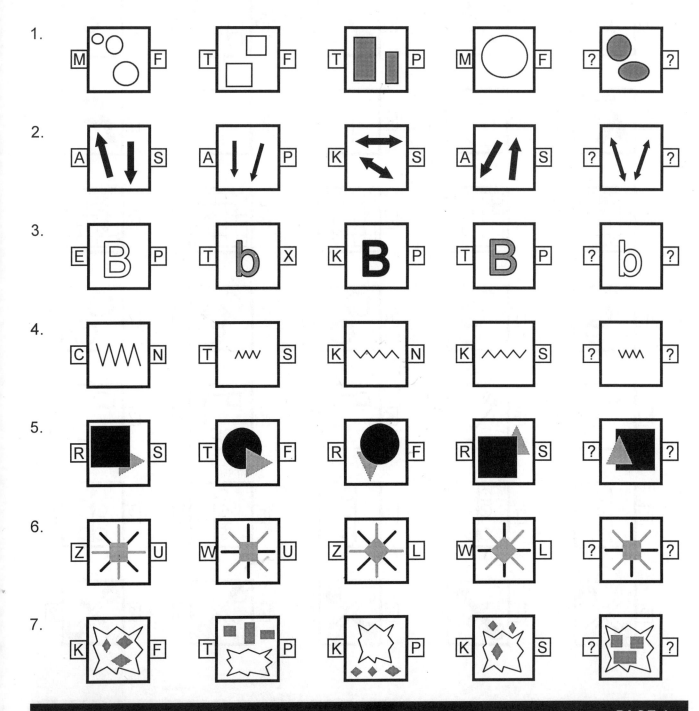

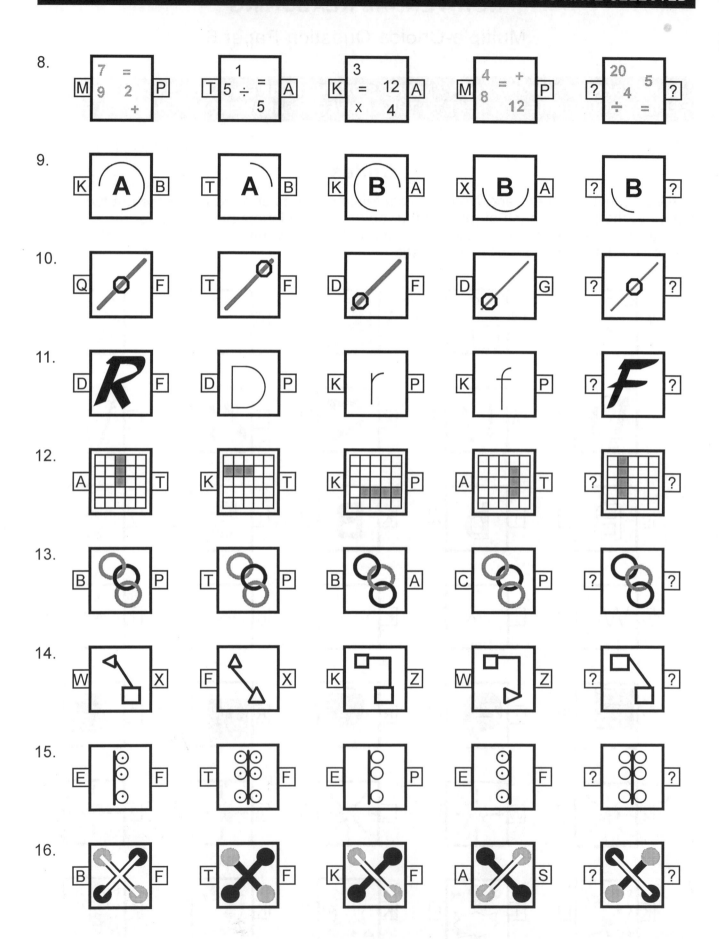

Time allowed - 9 mins

Serial Relationships

In each of the questions below there are five boxes on the left. The figures in these boxes are in order but one is missing. One of the figures in the boxes on the right is the missing figure.

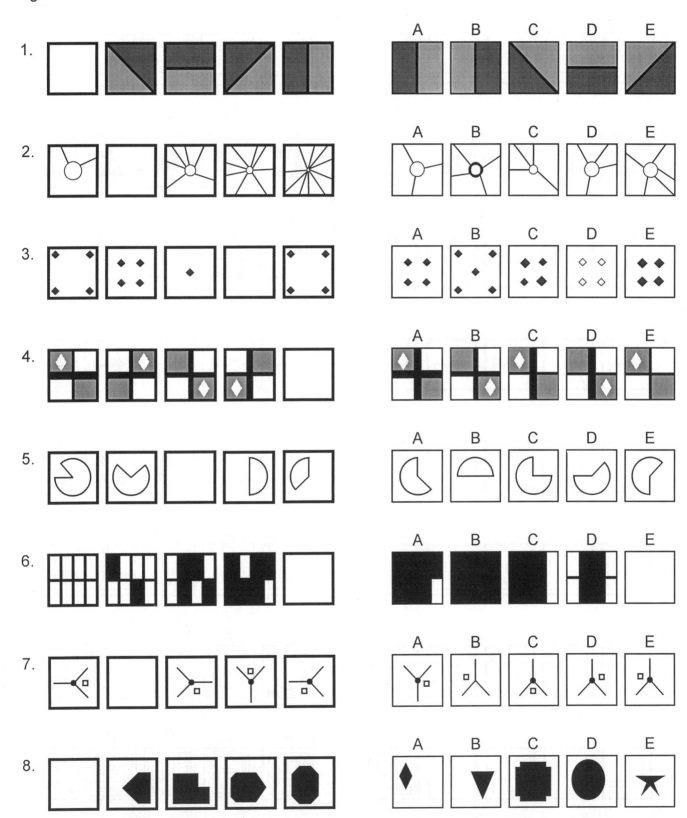

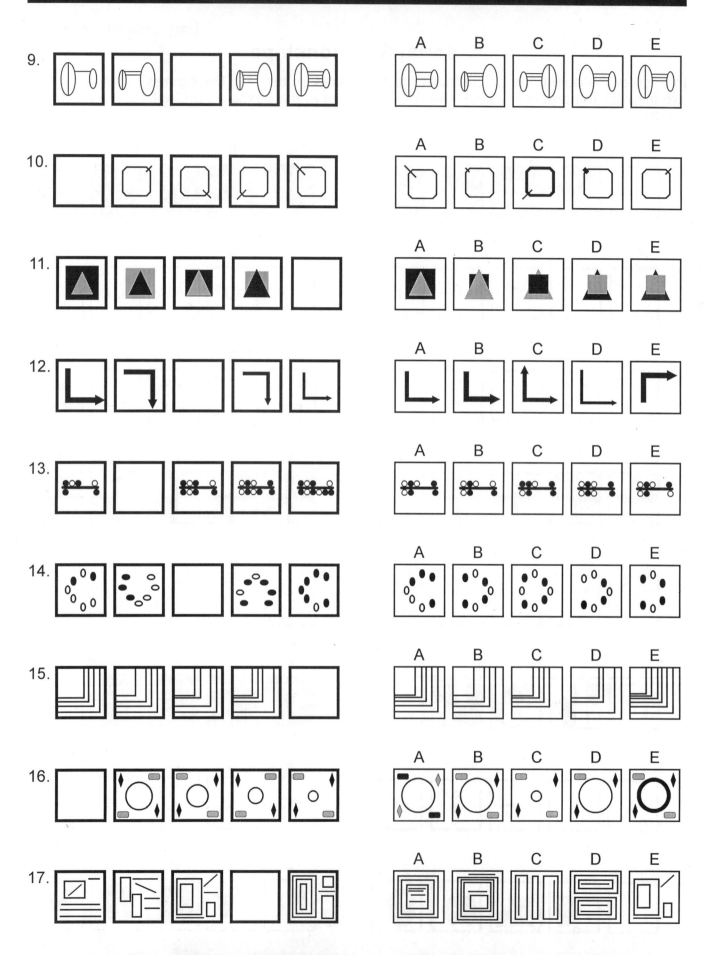

Copyright 1999   Athey Educational

Secondary Selection Portfolio

NON-VERBAL REASONING
Multiple-Choice Question Paper 5

REMEMBER TO RECORD YOUR ANSWERS ON THE ANSWER PAPER BY DRAWING A LINE THROUGH THE BOX NEXT TO THE ANSWER OR ANSWERS YOU HAVE SELECTED

Time allowed - 6 mins

Matrices

In each of the questions below there are four boxes on the left. Three of the boxes contain shapes or patterns. The fourth box is empty. There is a rule connecting the shapes or patterns in each row. There is also a rule for the columns. Work out the rules and choose A, B, C, D or E to show which is the missing shape or pattern.

1.   A   B   C   D   E

2.   A   B   C   D   E

3.   A   B   C   D   E

4.   A   B   C   D   E

5.   A   B   C   D   E

6.

A   B   C   D   E

7.

A   B   C   D   E

8.

A   B   C   D   E

9.

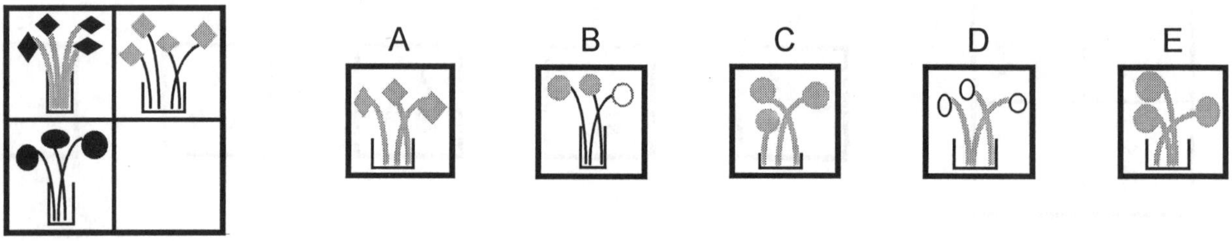

A   B   C   D   E

10.

A   B   C   D   E

11.

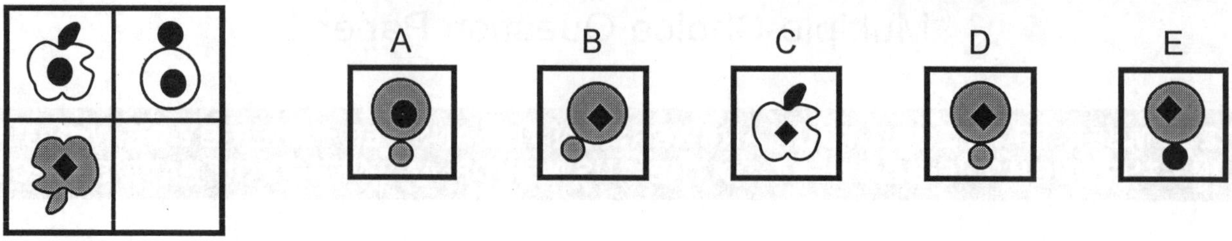

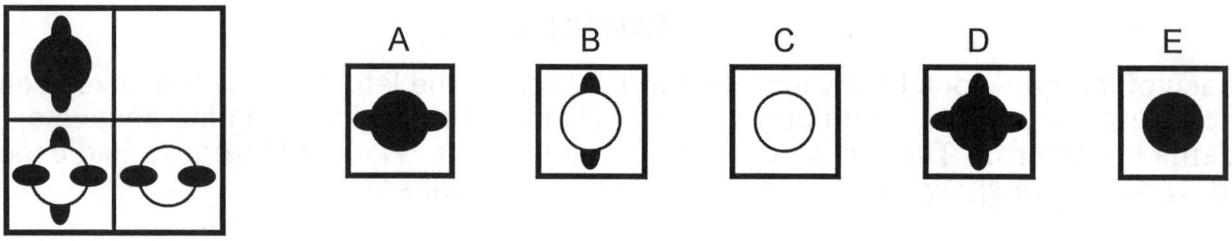

A   B   C   D   E

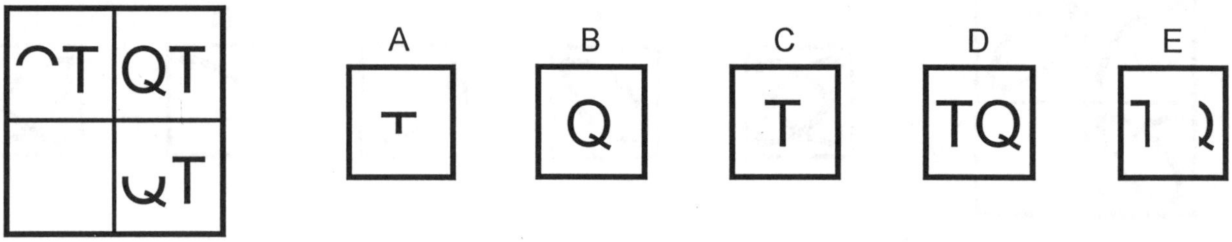

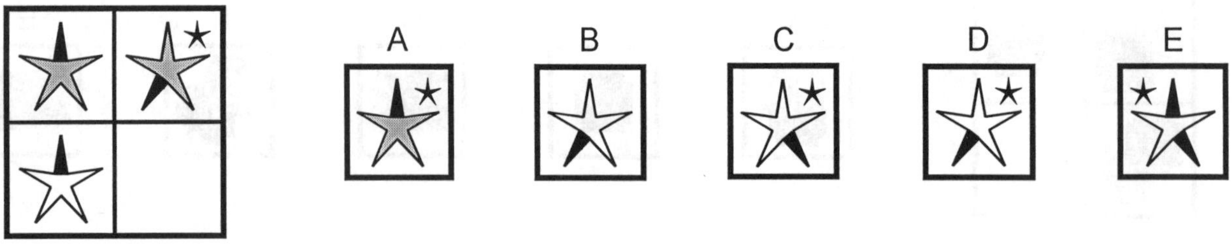

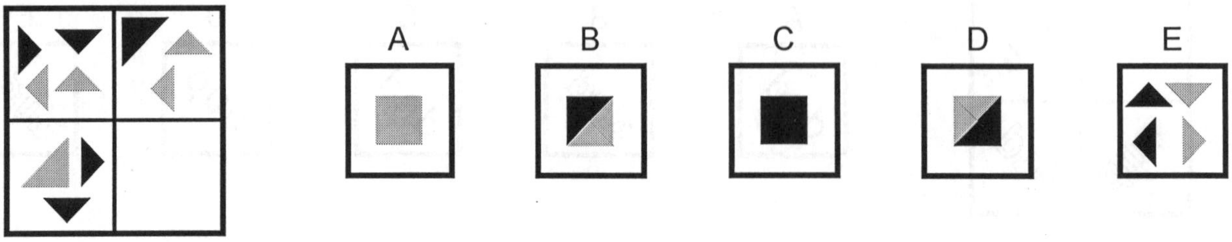

12.

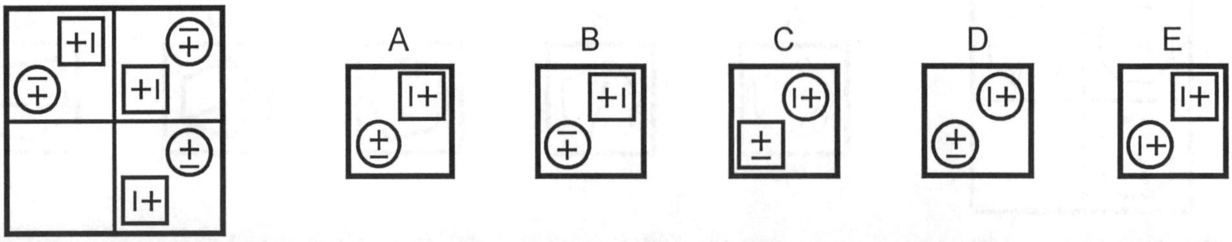

A   B   C   D   E

Time allowed - 7 mins

Isomorphic Relationships

In each of these questions the figures in the first three boxes are similar in some way.
Look at the shapes in boxes A to G and find **TWO** shapes which are similar to the first
three shapes.

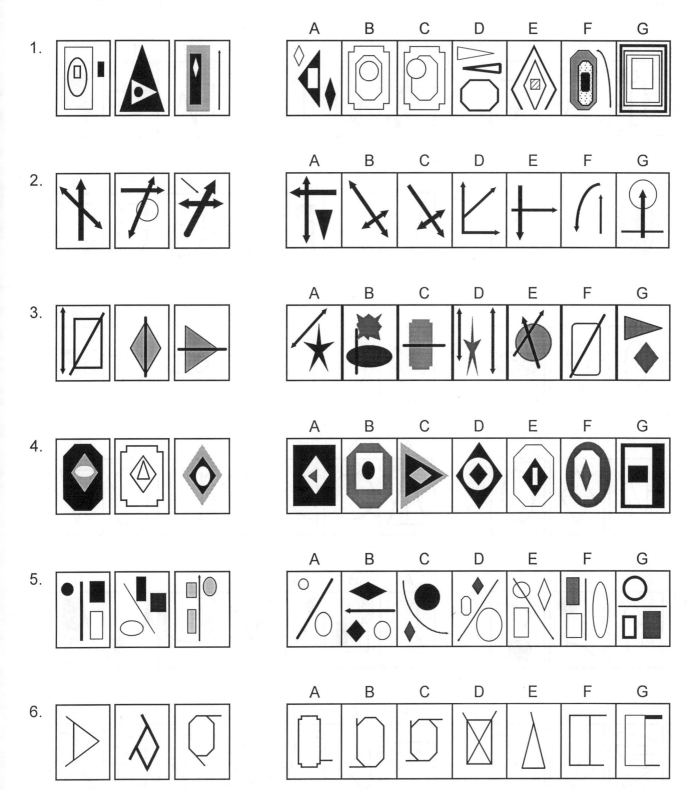

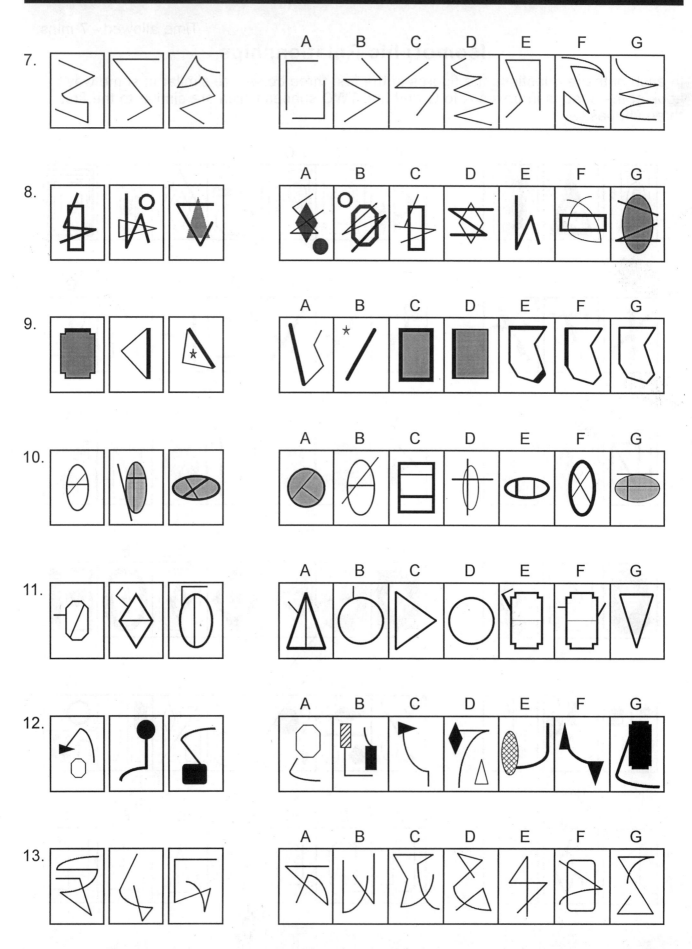